Three Wagons West

Three Wagons West

Adventures on the Oregon Trail

George W. Maybee

Copyright © 2014 by George W. Maybee.

Library of Congress Control Number:		2014910495
ISBN:	Hardcover	978-1-4990-3266-6
	Softcover	978-1-4990-3268-0
	eBook	978-1-4990-3262-8

All rights reserved. No part of this book may be reproduced or transmitted in any form or by any means, electronic or mechanical, including photocopying, recording, or by any information storage and retrieval system, without permission in writing from the copyright owner.

Any people depicted in stock imagery provided by Thinkstock are models, and such images are being used for illustrative purposes only.
Certain stock imagery © Thinkstock.

This book was printed in the United States of America.

Rev. date: 06/05/2014

To order additional copies of this book, contact:
Xlibris LLC
1-888-795-4274
www.Xlibris.com
Orders@Xlibris.com
627908

CONTENTS

Leaving Home 9

The Trail Begins 18

North to Nebraska 24

Prairie Dogs, Rattle Snakes and Coyotes 31

Beyond the Bluffs 40

The Promised Land 46

At Home in Oregon 53

Oh give me a home with a river nearby,
Where the trees stand tall,
And craggy mountains touch the sky.

LEAVING HOME

"Charlie! What about the baby?"

"The baby will be all right. We won't leave until it's big enough."

Mary folded her arms and turned away, shaking her head. She couldn't accept pulling up roots so dearly gained. Her face flared red and she thought of the children. Clara and Charles would miss their schooling.

"You always say school is so important," she said as she whirled to face him. "Why not just move to the city?"

"We're not city people. I want us to have room to spread out, a place where I can work and we can all grow."

"I just think it's too much. I don't want to drag the children clear across the country." Her voice quavered and she trembled. She was close to crying when she said as surely as she could, "I won't do it!" Charles went to the window and looked out. He was in no mood to argue.

"Get me some coffee and let me think." She went to the stove and brought the pot. He sat down at the table. She poured the coffee and sat down across from him.

"I hate fighting, but this is crazy," she said. "It's too far and too dangerous." He looked at the wall and shook his head.

9

"It's not crazy! The roads are safe now. It's a chance for a better life." He finished his cup without another word and went outside.

It was the summer of 1876, and times were tough in the township of Agnes, Kansas. Charles Maybee's small farm produced barely enough to feed his family. His part-time profession as a carpenter brought in a little spending money, but he was tired of scraping through. He wanted to pick up and leave for greener pastures. With four children and a pregnant wife, he felt trapped. When he first came to Kansas, he prospered enough to buy a farm and start a family. Now, ten years later, the family included Clara, Charles, George and Alice. Clara was eight and Charles was six. Little George was three and Alice was two. They were a happy flock, and his wife, Mary Jane, was content where they were. She couldn't believe Charles was serious about going two thousand miles to an uncertain future in Oregon.

He was sick of Kansas, sick of hard times. He leaned against the barn and watched a hawk circle over the field. It seemed so free and in control. He imagined going alone, and sending for Mary after he had a place. It would be easier for him, but he knew he couldn't leave her to bring the children. He felt like it was all or nothing. The hawk swooped down and snatched up something. He watched it fly up and disappear behind the barn. After a smoke, he went into the house and started again.

"I don't want to fight either, but we're going." Mary said nothing. Usually calm and understanding, but fiercely stubborn, she had never been so frustrated. Even being disowned by her father for marrying a "Damn Yankee" wasn't this bad. She withdrew and moped around the house. Not unlike her father, Charles was a commanding man, rock-hard and short on words. They had never been at such odds before. She couldn't hide it from the children. They felt her unhappiness and didn't understand. She thought Charles wouldn't go without her, but she wasn't sure. They barely spoke to each other and their unspoken thoughts bore down like heavy yokes. The children took on their gloom.

One day Clara heard little Alice crying in the bedroom and went in. Mary was holding Alice and sobbing. She sat on the bed beside them and they all cried.

"Mama, what's wrong with you and Daddy?" Mary wiped her eyes and pulled the girl close.

"It's because Daddy wants to go to Oregon."

"Why does he want us to go?"

"He thinks we'll like it there. He means well." Clara pressed against her mother. Mary rocked them until they stopped crying.

"It will be alright," she whispered. "It will be alright."

A week passed, and then another, before Charles mentioned Oregon again. She didn't say much. Oregon was driving them apart. They were badly upset, having thoughts they had never dreamed before. Still, he was determined to go and began making serious plans.

It had been twenty years since he left New York to prospect for gold in California. Strong, determined and resourceful, he prospected for ten years throughout the west. Roaming from gold camp to gold camp, he made a modest living but never struck it big. At times he worked at carpentry, building school houses in little towns and saving money for another try in the goldfields. Traveling by horseback across Oregon, he fished in its clear rivers, and hunted deer in its virgin forests. He was on his way home when he nearly froze during the brutal Montana winter of 1865. The following spring he flirted with death making his way down the Missouri River on a raft. In Saint Joseph, Missouri, he turned into a hospital, weak and gaunt, racked with river fever. It was there that he met Mary Jane, the pretty young nurse who helped him recover. They fell in love and were married in June, 1866. He took his bride to Kansas where they settled near his mother's sister, Aunt Jenny. But now he wanted to move on.

The urge to leave Kansas and go west had been building all year. Neighbors Bill Jenkins and Tom Brown were like-minded. Halfway convinced that Mary would go along with his plans after the baby was born, Charles met with them to talk in earnest about homesteading in Oregon. Jenkins was a big easy-going Texan who ran cattle on land that bordered the Maybee farm. His hopes for doing better in Kansas were gone. He shared Charles' desire to find a better place to farm and raise his family. Brawny Tom Brown kept milk cows, raised chickens and grew corn down the road from Jenkins. He too was fed up with life in Kansas. Charles believed that Oregon was a land of opportunity where they would be sure to make good. His neighbors knew about his adventures in the west and respected his opinion. The three men mulled over their prospects and reached a friendly agreement. They hatched a plan to sell out and head for the fertile farmlands of Oregon. They understood that the trip would be hard, but they were confident they could do it. Thousands of families had gone before. With a handshake, they committed themselves to making the journey.

"Now comes the hard part," Charles told them. "Get your wives to agree, and we'll be on our way."

A week later Bill and Tom came to tell Charles that their wives were okay with it. They went out to the barn and had a drink on it. They agreed to pool their resources and help each other get ready to go. In the weeks ahead, Charles studied a yellowed copy of a journal written about the Oregon Trail during the peak of westward emigration in the 1850s. Details about the trail, what to take, and how to outfit a wagon were all there. He poured over the journal until he knew it by heart. He spent long hours outfitting his farm wagon for overland travel. He went into the woods and cut a bundle of maple saplings. In the barn he laid them out for trimming. Green and flexible, they were perfect for making hoops to support a canvas covering, the roof of the wagon. He cut five matching pairs and trimmed them flat at the base. Each pole tapered from about two inches at the base to less than an inch at the tip. Evenly spaced on both sides of the wagon, he attached five poles to the base boards. Then he bent opposing poles to overlap in the middle of the wagon and tied them together with strong twine and strips of leather. He also cut poles for an undercarriage and made a frame to support a canvas bed to carry firewood, tent poles and a spare wheel.

Baby Janet was born in early December. She was a sweet little thing with a powerful set of lungs that kept the family aware of her needs. Bill's wife, Rosemary, and Tom's wife, Janie, came to see the baby and help take care of the household while Mary recovered. They talked about the plans their husbands were making. Would they really be going to Oregon? Mary was still uncommitted.

"I just know I won't go anywhere until my baby is ready. Even then, what about the hundreds of miles out there where anything can happen?" she said.

Along with a string of cattle and two small children, Bill and Rosemary had driven a wagon loaded with their belongings all the way from Texas.

"We had our troubles, but we got stronger and sometimes we had fun," Rosemary told them. They listened closely while she described the sometimes exciting, sometimes frightening, days and nights she had experienced along the trail to Kansas.

"I think we can make a good trip out of it," Rosemary said. "And I really want to see the west."

"I know," Mary said. "Charlie has told me about it for years, but it's so hard to get there."

As winter deepened, Mary thought more and more about the possibility of going to Oregon. She rocked little Janet by the fire as the winds whistled and snow swirled across the field where Clara and her little brother Charles played. As Janet grew stronger, Mary would sometimes lay her on a blanket before the hearth where she gurgled as Clara and Alice rolled her around. She thought about spring and sunny days when she could carry Janet around the farm.

Mary's resistance thawed with the melting snow. Baby Janet was a lively bundle and her mother was proud. She began telling the children they might be moving when school was out. She talked about going to Oregon with their friends. Son Charles went to the same little schoolhouse with his sister Clara. They walked together and he looked to her for answers about things.

"What is Oregon?" he asked her.

"Daddy told me about it. He was there before." she told him.

"What is it?"

"It's a place with big trees and mountains with snow on them. And there's rivers and lakes everywhere." she said.

"Oh. Why are we going there?"

"Mama says we'll have a new house and a big farm with horses and apple trees."

"How can we go there?"

"Daddy's fixing our wagon to ride. We can camp in a tent and have fun."

As the spring flowers bloomed, Mary got the courage to tell Charles she would go. He wrapped her in his arms and kissed her face while the children watched. Radiant with energy and joy, they plunged into the work of preparing to travel. Mary began choosing clothing and household items they would take and setting things aside that could stay behind.

Charles was nearly finished working on the wagon and getting anxious to try it on the road. He put hooks on the hoops to use for hanging things, and built other attachments to carry supplies, tools and spare parts. Now he needed a team of oxen to pull it. Jenkins used two pairs coming up from Texas and advised Charles that it was the best way to go.

"They're slower than horses or mules, but they got the strength you need for the long haul," he said. "And they can live on the trail grasses. Don't need to carry grain for them."

Charles traded his goats, one of his horses and most of his farm equipment for the oxen and learned how to work them. Jenkins showed him some tricks and he practiced driving them around the field.

When he had mastered driving the oxen, he loaded up the whole family and started down the road to Jenkins's place.

"It won't be like this on the trail," he told Mary. "We'll have the wagon full of things and most of the time you'll be walking." Jenkins came out from the porch when they pulled up.

"Lookin' good there, Charlie." His boys, Ron and Bob, ran out and climbed up to squeeze in beside little Charles and George. "I'll take 'em down to Tom's and back," Charles said.

"Okay, Charlie, see you."

As the days edged toward summer, it was humid and stormy. Sometimes the children spent the night on the floor in their parents' room. One night they lay awake while the house creaked in the wind and hail pounded on the roof. In the morning Charles went out and scanned the sky. It had stopped raining and black clouds hung low over the field. It was very quiet and then it started. A huge funnel twisted out of the clouds. It raced toward Charles, churning up everything in its path. He ran for the door and yelled at Mary.

"Get the kids to the cellar! It's a tornado!" He ran in and grabbed pillows and blankets while Mary and the children ran into the cellar.

Clara screamed, "Where's Snoopy!" Charles called and Snoopy came running from under the porch. When they were all tucked into a cocoon he pulled down the cellar door and came to them. They held tight and then it was over. The roar passed to the south and they were spared. The back fence was gone and some shingles were missing, but nothing more. The animals were all standing by the barn. Jenkins came out fine but the roof of Tom's chicken house was gone and his corn crop was ruined. They all got together at Jenkins' house to count their blessings. Charles said he didn't think they had tornadoes in Oregon.

"Let's drink to that!" the Texan said as he raised his glass. And they drank with pleasure.

On May 24, 1877, the three families loaded their wagons and started up the road to the Oregon Trail. Mary took a long last look at the empty house and held back tears as they rolled out the gate. Baby Janet cried and Alice whined, but the older children were excited and eager to go. She held Janet to her breast while Alice nestled in her lap and little George sat in a nook between boxes of goods stacked behind the seat. The older children walked behind the wagon. Black and white Snoopy ran ahead exploring all the sights and smells. Master Charles walked beside the wagon and led the oxen with verbal commands and cracks of a whip. Two horses and a cow trailed behind and a cage of hens was strapped to one side of the wagon. For better or worse, Charles and his family were bound for the promised land of Oregon.

The Oregon Trail

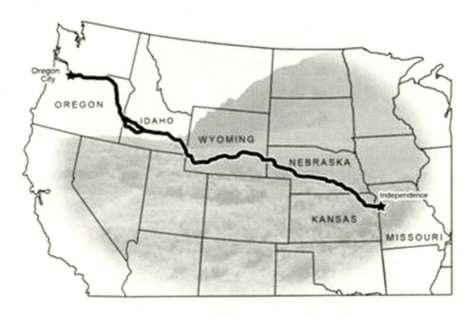

*From Independence, Missouri, to Oregon City,
Oregon, the Oregon Trail cut across Kansas, Nebraska,
Wyoming, Idaho and Oregon.
Idaho and Wyoming were part of the Territory of Idaho when
Charles and Mary Jane traveled to Oregon in 1877.*

THE TRAIL BEGINS

The first day on the road was tempered with sentimental feelings, hopeful expectations and rough awakenings. The wagons bumped along and Mary was glad to get down and carry baby Janet. Clara took Alice by the hand and walked with Mary behind the wagon. The boys walked close to Charles, always looking to see what was ahead. Mostly it was plain old rolling countryside with occasional farm buildings and animals back off the road. Coming along at a comfortable distance behind were the wagons of Bill and Tom. Bill had a string of cattle and behind the cattle came Tom.

It was noon before Charles pulled off the road into an open field near a creek. He turned the animals loose to drink and graze. Young Charles blazed the way through grass as tall as little George to explore the creek. Bill pulled up and then Tom. Bill's boys, Ron and Bob, ran to the creek where young Charles and George were throwing rocks. Bill's big Labrador mutt ran ahead and jumped in the creek. Snoopy went in after him. The dogs came out shaking their coats and splashing the boys. Tom's daughter, Denise, went over to be with Clara.

Rosemary and Janie sat down on the grass with Mary. They opened the lunches, packed the night before, and called the men and boys. Everyone gathered around while flies zipped in for a share of the food.

"It's like they knew we were coming," Mary said.

"They always seem to," said Charles. They finished lunch and hitched up.

"How far since we left," Charles asked Jenkins. Bill had a roadometer on his wagon and went to check it. He opened the gearbox attached to the rear wheel hub and read the scale.

"Reads about six and a half," he said. "Not a bad start."

"So, if we double that today, and do better tomorrow, we can reach Dragoon Creek tomorrow night."

"Should do," said Bill. Charles noted the date and distance in his log: May 24, 1877 – first stop, 6.5 miles.

As the day wore on, the children wore down and the women were anxious. With the sinking sun, Charles studied the countryside looking for a little lake where he had fished a few times. He saw the lake off to the left and called to Mary.

"We'll camp here," he said. "I'm starving." He turned into a spot well worn by other travelers and lit a smoke while the others pulled in.

Making camp was a routine they needed to learn. Rosemary and Bill led the way, but it took a good hour before they had things in order and the animals tended. Charles unloaded part of the wagon to make space where Mary and the little girls could sleep. With the wagons arranged in the shape of a "U" and the tents in a line to enclose the space, they made a fire and the women started supper. It was near dark before they ate. Tired to the bone, everyone got ready for bed as the moon rose over the lake.

The camp came alive at daybreak. The men rolled out and got a fire going. Charles' legs were a little stiff at first and his right shoulder was sore. He stretched to loosen up.

"Thought I was in better shape," he said.

"Me too," said Tom.

"Yeah." Bill said. "Took me near a week to settle in comin' from Texas."

The women got breakfast ready while they rounded up the animals, took down the tents and reloaded the wagons. Bill checked the roadometer.

"Made eleven miles," he said. Charles shrugged and logged it in his book.

"Got to do better today," he said. The smell of wood smoke and frying bacon drew them to the fireside. Around the fire with hot coffee and heaps of bread, bacon and eggs, the families chattered and compared aches and pains. There were lots of sore feet. The children were jumping with energy and ate like little wolves. Finished eating, young Charles went to the lake with Ron and Bob to get buckets of water. Everything was cleaned up, the fire was doused, and Charles led his wagon onto the road.

Yesterday's shakedown had been a good test. He drove ahead, whistling and watching while the dogs romped in and out of the tall grass beside the road. Mary rode in the wagon with Alice and Janet. The boys walked behind with Clara. Two men on horses approached from the north and Charles stopped to ask about the road ahead.

"Bridge out on the creek about five miles up, easy to ford," one rider said.

"Thanks neighbor," Charles said as they rode away. The road was hard and rocky, the wagons riding rough as they continued north. He walked carefully to keep from stepping on sharp rocks. His feet hurt.

In the heat of the day they reached the creek with the washed-out bridge. Charles saw where flood waters had surged and left tree limbs and brush scattered along the banks. The bridge footing had torn loose on one end and water crested up over the fallen timbers. It was hot and humid. They decided to ford the creek and then have lunch. The water was shallow near the bank, but deepened toward the middle and the current was fast. Charles mounted King, his big sorrel, and rode into the creek to let him drink. Then he carried the older children across the creek, one by one. The little ones stayed in the wagon with Mary. Ten yards upstream from the bridge there was a good crossing. He rode beside the wagon and drove it to the water, waiting while the oxen drank. The creek bottom was firm and the oxen easily pulled the wagon to the other side. Water dripped from the wagon wheels as it rolled up the bank and onto grassy level ground. The children were at the edge of the creek with the dogs, splashing in the cold water. It was very hot. Charles went to the creek and splashed with them. Then he brought a bucket of water up for Mary.

It was a slow process, but everyone got across without trouble. They gathered in a clump of trees near the creek and rested in the shade while they ate lunch.

"Slow start, but I felt better once we got going," Charles said. "Reckon we may not make the Dragoon today."

"Don't matter," said Tom. "We'll get there when we get there."

"Right true," said Bill. With all accounted for and a good lunch to go on, they left the creek behind.

That night they were a little faster making camp and took their time relaxing around the fire after supper. Tired and dirty, Janie wished she were home where she could clean up and sleep in her bed. The sky was gray and the still air gave no relief. Sore feet, humid heat and mosquito bites had everyone miserable, and the children were cranky. Rosemary kept a positive attitude. She felt sure things would get better and laughed about tripping and falling face down in the dirt when they were making camp. With the time lost at the washed-out bridge, they had only traveled about eight miles. Charles figured they would surely get to Dragoon Creek the next day. Mary soothed the children, wiping a cool damp cloth on their faces before they went to bed. A welcome wind came up in the night and rain drops fell steadily on the tents and wagon tops. It was a good sleeping rain.

The rain stopped sometime before daylight. The men were first to rise. They sloshed through mud and wet grass to gather wood for a fire. With the fire going, the women drug themselves out and started breakfast. They complained of soreness and feeling tired. Mary's American Rubber Company shoes were stiff and a little tight, but she was glad they kept her feet dry. The children all had comfortable rubber boots. They were very hungry and crowded together by the fire watching their mothers cook. Clara rocked baby Janet in her arms and kissed her hair. The men finished packing and lingered over hot coffee, biscuits and bacon. While the women cleaned up, the men checked their wagons and yoked the oxen.

Mud puddles stood in the road and the boys splashed through them. Charles rode King. It was cool, and fog hung over the fields. Misty gray and mysterious, trees bordered the backs of fields. Sometimes the mud was bad and there were spots where the wheels sank down and the oxen strained to pull the wagons. When the sun lifted the fog it got steamy and hot. Charles cut their noontime short. He wanted to reach the Dragoon and cross to the Santa Fe Trail before the day was out.

"Got to keep moving," he told Mary. The road was better in the afternoon and Mary got down to walk. She stood holding Janet until the Jenkins' wagon reached her and then she walked with Rosemary. They took turns holding Janet and time passed quickly while they talked. The wagons kept a good pace, but in the twilight, still short of the Dragoon, they pulled off and made camp.

Up early and on the road before sunrise, they reached Dragoon Creek in less than an hour. The water was low enough for an easy crossing. Charles logged their location: May 27 -- Santa Fe Trail at Dragoon. A marker pointing to the east read:

Topeka 30 Miles. The road was well traveled and several westbound wagons passed while they crossed the creek and started toward Topeka.

"Better road here," Charles said. "Should make Topeka in good time." They traveled a few miles to the northeast and stopped for lunch.

They were 47 miles from home by the end of the day and beginning to settle into an efficient routine. The next day they camped on the outskirts of Topeka, where the Oregon Trail branched off from the Santa Fe Trail. In the morning, they stopped in Topeka on the way to the bridge that crossed the Arkansas River. They parked near a farmers market, and the men greased their wagon wheels and filled their water barrels with fresh well water while the women shopped for fresh fruit and vegetables. Further along, they stopped at a general store. Charles bought boot oil, a gallon of good whiskey and two boxes of cigars. Mary bought new shoes and jars of hard candy for the children. Crossing the bridge, Mary looked down at the brown water. They still had over a hundred miles to go just to reach Nebraska, but the river seemed like the end of Kansas, the end of home. Charles saw it differently.

NORTH TO NEBRASKA

The Oregon Trail angled to the northwest coming away from Topeka. It was easier walking and the three families settled into a fairly strict routine. Their days began at first light and they were making better mileage. They usually stopped to rest and eat around ten in the morning. They were stronger and able to enjoy seeing new countryside. The children helped with setting up camp, finding firewood, carrying water and taking care of the little ones. Young Charles was entrusted to keep an eye on the chickens when they were turned loose to hunt. Around the evening fire there was much talk about the day's events and what was expected ahead. In three days they reached the Vermillion River and crossed in time to make camp before dark It was the first of June and they had come 107 miles. After supper, Charles opened a box of his cigars and sat smoking with Tom and Bill while they sampled his whiskey.

"We better get some more of this before we get too far," Bill said.

"Best we do," Charles said. "Won't be any out there on the prairie." They toasted the idea with another round of whiskey.

As daylight faded, flashes lit the dark clouds to the west and soon a burst of wind swept through the camp. Ashes flew into Charles' face and flames torched above the hot coals. They finished their drinks and began putting things up for the night.

The clouds moved in and thunder boomed before everyone was under cover. They lay in their blankets and listened to the roaring rain, the wind whipping the canvas tents and lashing against the wagons.

All through the night it rained and it was cold and wet in the morning. It was still raining when Charles looked out from the tent. The river was a boiling torrent and the camp ground was a mass of puddles and mud. Damn good we got across before this, he thought. They stayed the day in camp and kept under cover. Mary read to the children from her book of Aesop's Fables. They ate apples and bread and she let them have a piece of candy. The rain stopped in the afternoon and the men got a fire going. Big helpings of bacon, beans and bread raised their spirits. They stayed close to the fire, drying their damp clothes. That night the moon came out, silver and bright.

Under the clear morning sky, they broke camp and continued moving to the northwest. The Big Blue River intersected the trail fifty miles ahead. Three days later they camped near the river at Alcove Spring. It was a beautiful spot where travelers usually stopped to rest before going on to cross the river. They gladly agreed – they needed a good rest and time to wash clothes and perform maintenance on the wagons. It was like a little vacation and Mary woke up smiling, happy to be there. After breakfast, she and the boys went to the spring for water while Clara stayed with Alice and Janet. A path led from the road down a gentle hill to the spring. They started down the path, the boys scrambling ahead. At the same time, a woman in gingham started up the path with her daughter, their blond hair shining, their eyes on the path. They each carried a bucket of water. As the boys ran past, the girl stumbled and water splashed from her bucket. The woman pulled her up and they came ahead. Mary watched closely. The woman looked familiar.

"I'm sorry," Mary said as they met on the path. "My boys are too frisky." Face to face, Mary realized she knew the woman.

"Gloria?" she said. The woman's face opened into a bright smile.

"Mary! Mary Jane Mount? I can't believe it!"

"I can't either. It's been so many years." The woman set down her bucket and stepped forward to hug Mary.

"This is my daughter, Jenny," she said. Jenny smiled and took Mary's outstretched hand.

"I knew you got married and went to Kansas. Never dreamed I'd see you out here like this. Where are you going?" Gloria said.

"Going to Oregon, how about you?"

"We're going to California with friends from Kansas City. You've got to meet my husband Jack and them." They stood in the middle of the path for a long time, talking about the days when they were schoolmates in St. Joseph and everything that had happened since. Gloria's daughter was a year younger than Clara, and her son, Roger, was about George's age. She had lost one son at birth two years ago. Jack had come from Council Bluff to work at the mill in St. Joe when he met Gloria. The prospect of going west had fascinated him ever since he was a boy reading about the great migration that followed the California gold rush.

Back at the wagon, Mary told Charles about Gloria and they walked over to meet her and her husband, Jack Jarrett. The Jarrett wagon was nested together with three others. Gloria waved and walked out to meet them.

"Glad to meet you, ma'am," Charles said. "Mary says you went to school with her in St. Joe. She showed me that school one time."

"Mary told me about you too. And I'm very glad to meet you," she said. "Come and sit awhile. Jack is out getting firewood." Gloria and Jack had organized their group and assumed leadership for the trip. They had saved and planned for the day they would all travel to California and settle in the Sacramento Valley. Gloria had been reluctant at first, but Jack's enthusiasm won her over. She got her friends, Virginia, Melissa and Gertrude excited about going and here they were, two weeks out of Kansas City, on the first leg of the great Oregon-California Trail.

Jack was a cheerful man with friendly dark eyes and an easy laugh. His confidence was catchy and his burley body let you believe he could handle most anything. He had worked at carpentry for 18 years and spoke the same language as Charles. They stood by the wagon and talked about using their trade skills to get a start in the west and acquire some good farm land. Traveling together would make their journey safer and they agreed to see if the other families were interested.

"We're going to stay here a few days, so we can leave together if you want to wait," Charles said.

"Sounds alright, Charlie, I'll let you know this afternoon." The two wives looked on with approval.

On the way back to their wagon, Charles told Mary he was sure Bill and Tom would go for joining the others. She agreed and went to tell Rosemary and Janie while Charles talked with the men. It was settled quickly. If the other party was willing, they would be glad to have them come along.

Charles strung a clothes line for Mary and sat oiling his boots while she hung the clothes, fresh and clean. Charles was in a thoughtful mood. He usually didn't say much about things, but he wanted to tell Mary how he felt. He thought about what he was putting her and the children through. It was a hard road, but it was a good road, and it would take them to a better place. The promise of Oregon drove him on.

"We will never pass this way again," he said. "It's hard going, but we'll make it. We're strong together. We'll forget the heat and the bugs. We'll remember the good parts and someday we'll remember today. And whatever happens we always have each other."

She turned and said, "I hope so, Charlie. I really hope so." He set down the boot he was working on and looked up.

"I love you, Mary Jane. I don't want to live without you. You know that, don't you?" Mary stopped hanging clothes and came to Charles.

"Yes, Charles Maybee, and you know I love *you*." They stood together, gently rocking in each other's arms.

"I'll make some room in the wagon," he said.

That afternoon Charles trimmed his beard and washed himself in the cold creek water that flowed from the spring pond. The cold water felt good in the hot sun.

"Jack came by when you were at the spring," Mary said.

"They're ready to go when we are. I told him we wanted to stay another day and he said that was fine. He seems like a good man."

"Good. I'll tell Bill and Tom."

"I thought we could have a big lunch or something so we could meet everybody."

"Alright, I'm for that. Maybe we could roast one of the chickens for our part. They're mighty fat from all those grass hoppers."

It was crowded in the wagon, but they didn't mind. The little ones were tucked in and sleeping soundly. The faint glow of moonlight filtered through the canvas, and a light breeze cooled the air inside the wagon. They listened to the frogs as they lay quietly, whispering. It was the first time they had spent the night together on the trail – the hard days and nights didn't matter now. The children were on top of them in the morning and they loved it.

Mary visited all the wagons and invited the wives to meet and decide what they would bring for lunch. They all got busy while the men set up a place in the shade where they could sit down together. By lunch time folks were already getting to know one another. The children were excited about the big doings and they ran around playing hide and seek with their new friends. It was a happy crowd that sat down to share a lunch that included the best each family had to offer. The men traded information about the Oregon Trail and what to expect along the way. They discussed the upcoming river crossing. The Big Blue was the largest tributary of the Arkansas River. It was dangerous to ford in high water, but they knew it was safe during periods of low water and agreed they would ford it to avoid the toll bridge fees if conditions were right. Charles pressed the argument for fording the river. It was the biggest river they would have to negotiate until they crossed the Platte River in western Nebraska, and Charles thought it would be good to test their wagons before they got that far.

The next day they broke camp and drove to the river with Charles leading the way. On the way to Oregon in the 1840s, Dr. Marcus Whitman had led a thousand emigrants across the river from the place where Charles stopped his wagon. It had been named Independence Crossing after the trail that led from Independence, Missouri. Now, more than thirty years after Dr. Whitman, Charles was confident he could lead his wagons across and on to the same destination. He mounted King and rode into the river to measure the depth, confirming that the water was low enough to allow their wagons to cross safely. The crossing was refreshing, even exhilarating, and a good bath for the animals. And Charles learned an important lesson. The caulking between the floor boards of his wagon had become dry and cracked and water surged up through the cracks. Some of the other wagons had the same problem. Now was the time to make repairs and avoid worse trouble down the road. From that day forward, he would periodically check the seals on his wagon.

That night the seven-wagon train was arranged in a polygon that enclosed an open space for tents and room where everyone could congregate. They were a spirited group, telling stories and laughing loudly around the fire.

The trail continued northwesterly along the Little Blue River, a fork that joined the Big Blue south of Independence Crossing. In two days they passed a stone marker designating the Nebraska state line. The trail continued in the general direction of the Little Blue. They would soon enter the short grass prairies of the Platte River Valley.

PRAIRIE DOGS, RATTLE SNAKES AND COYOTES

The seven wagons rolled into the small town of Fairbury a day after entering Nebraska. Fairbury, located on the Little Blue River, was a shipping center in the 1870s. A Union Pacific railroad line ran between Fairbury and Grand Island, Nebraska. Hundreds of train cars loaded with grain were shipped from Fairbury. The party shopped for fresh supplies to fill their stores for the long trek across the prairie. Jenkins found a store with spirits for sale. He and Tom loaded up with whiskey and wine and Charles added to his whiskey supply. One man from the Jarrett party went to a blacksmith to shoe his horse. The others went on to set up camp outside of town.

From Fairbury, they traveled through the valley of the Little Blue. Charles loaded his undercarriage with firewood from along the river bank and he caught fish for supper. Antelope herds sometimes crossed their path and Melissa's husband, James McClary, shot one to roast and share with the party. The extremely difficult and dangerous times of early travel on the Oregon Trail had faded into history. In 1864 there had been killings and property destruction by angry bands of Arapahoe, Kiowa and Sioux Indians. The trail had become a thoroughfare

31

for hundreds of freight wagons and the Indians struck against the invasion of their buffalo hunting grounds. By 1877, travel along the Little Blue was scenic and peaceful. The Indian raids were a thing of the past and there were many places to stop where good water and stores with a variety of supplies were available. After four days they left the river behind and continued northwest through sand hills into the Platte River Valley. Coming out of the hills, the flat open land spread before them like a great inland sea. The trail was wide and, at times, they traveled three and four abreast to avoid eating each other's dust. The territory was known as "The Coast of Nebraska" because the view across the shimmering sands while approaching the broad Platte River resembled the seashore of the Atlantic Ocean. The river, a network of overlapping channels, was up to two miles wide, the water shallow and muddy with particles of sand.

Two days travel and in the distance they could see the sandy beach-like banks of the Platte River. They continued to the west, following the river through the valley. The road was rutted with impressions left by the thousands of wagons and coaches that had passed before. They camped near a monument designating 32-mile creek. Once the location of a station where pony express riders stopped for rest and meals, it had been burned down during an Indian raid. The station was 32 miles east of the abandoned Fort Kearny, formerly operated to protect emigrants from Indian attacks and provide a safe place to rest and make repairs.

Wind-driven dust was a constant irritation. Mary made bandanas for the family, and this helped, but the children still got sand in their eyes. The wind often whipped up dust devils and the children were fascinated, but little George was afraid of them.

"Mama, what if those devils come here and catch us?" he asked.

"They can't catch us," Mary said. "They are just the wind playing games with the sand. They can't hurt us." Sometimes the dust devils did come close and the children learned to like them.

At first the children were frightened by the nightly chorus of yipping, howling coyotes, but they were soon able to fall asleep in the midst of the yowling. They loved seeing prairie dogs and tried to get close to them, but whenever a rattle snake showed itself they ran yelling to the wagon. Charles killed some of the snakes and grilled them to serve at supper.

The firewood that Charles collected along the Little Blue was long gone and, other than sage brush and yucca plants, there was nothing much to burn along the Platte River. He thought of the great forests in Oregon and the day when he would be there. He thought of the tall firs, the cool shade and fresh green undergrowth. There were trees on some of the islands in the Platte River, but quicksand generally blocked access to them. The buffalo herds had been drastically reduced by greedy hunters, but their droppings could still be found and used for fuel. Young Charles and little George were assigned to pick up any buffalo chips they saw along the way and put them into the undercarriage. An occasional bull was seen leading a thirsty string of cows and calves to the river. One afternoon they heard a rumble and, from a trough a hundred yards away, a small herd thundered up like a swell in the ocean and disappeared in another trough, rising again and finally disappearing in a cloud of dust.

They pressed to maximize their mileage, knowing travel would be slower when they reached Wyoming. Their progress was excellent until one day the weather changed and they made camp early to be ready for what looked like a serious storm moving in from the west. The clear blue sky turned dark in the distance and brilliant streaks of lightning flashed from the clouds. They could hear faint rumbles and a cooling wind swept through the camp.

"Big storm out there," Charles said. "Hope it stays away." The rumbles got louder and the wind stronger and everyone hurried to make sure their wagons and tents were secure. They herded the animals together inside the camp and got set for whatever might come. The light began to fade and the wind whistled through the camp as Charles stood watching the sky. He could smell rain and he leaned into the wind to keep from falling back.

"Mary!" He called. "This looks bad. I think we'd better all get together in the tent, away from the wagon. It could get pushed over."

"But the tent isn't as strong as the wagon. What if it blows over? She said.

"We need to be close to the ground where the wind can't knock us down, tent or no tent. The wagon is high and has more surfaces for the wind to push against. We will be safer in the tent."

"Are you sure?"

"I'm sure! Now come on before it's too late."

Mary handed the girls to Charles and got down from the wagon. They went to the tent and lay close together wrapped in their blankets. The wind began to roar and hail pounded the tent. They held on, hoping that the tent would stand up against the wind. The ground was white with balls of hail and the wind swelled the tent, pulling the ropes rigid and rattling the canvas. Then a downpour of heavy rain drenched everything and the tent poles moved in the ground. Suddenly the canvas sailed up and flew in the wind, held by one surviving pole. Charles jumped up and grabbed one of the tent poles. He pulled it down and jammed it into the wet sand. He leaned on the pole, twisting it and pushing with all his might. Mary moved into the corner under the sagging canvas, holding the children close around her. Charles pulled down another pole and forced it into the sand. It was enough to keep them out of the rain, and he sat down in the darkness, peering out into the rain when lightning struck. He prayed that the storm would pass and let them live. They heard a hollow thump and a shrill scream. In a flash of lightning Charles saw that one of the wagons had gone over. He got up, pushed his way past the animals, and staggered toward the fallen wagon. Each flash of light told him a little more. The wagon lay on its side, its canvas cover limp and torn. Jack was there, standing on the lee side of the wagon with his arm on the shoulders of Frank Robinson, Frank's arm around his wife, Virginia. They looked at Charles and shook their heads.

"We're alright, Charlie. Just one hell of a jolt," Frank said. They stood there in the dark, sopping wet but unhurt.

"Can't do much till this blows over," Jack said.

Charles waded back through the stinging rain. Mary sat with the children crowded around her, the canvas flapping up and down above them.

"They're alright," he said. "Just have to wait it out."

When daylight came, the wind had died and the sky was clear. The yellow sun appeared on the horizon, pushing long shadows across the flat prairie. The men got together at Robinson's wagon.

"That was no ordinary storm," Frank said. "I think we got brushed by a tornado."

"Sounded like one to me," Charles said. Mud ran down the side of the wagon as they raised it. The wagon swayed back and forth when the wheels hit the ground. The canvas was ripped away from the baseboard in a few places, but the frame had not been damaged. Everything was a jumble inside and Virginia got in to sort things out.

"Lucky we didn't bust a wheel with all the weight on that side when she went over," Frank said. Virginia yelled down from the wagon.

"Lucky we didn't bust our heads!"

Charles went with Tom and Bill to round up the cattle that had wandered off. It was time for lunch when they got back and they hadn't had breakfast, but they had all the cattle with them. The rest of the day was spent drying blankets and clothes and putting the camp in order. Charles checked the roadometer and logged the mileage – June 20, 360 miles, bad storm, lost day and a half. Around the fire at sundown, everyone gave thanks and talked of better days ahead. Charles passed his jug around and there was much happy laughter and loud singing. All was well again.

The prairie stretched ahead with no end in sight and the days seemed ever longer. But things changed for the better when they saw a green field ahead near the river.

"Looks like a farm," Charles said. They came to a roadside shack with bushels of corn stacked high under a rickety roof. An old man stood to greet them and they stopped, overjoyed to see this out-of-the-way market. Charles stepped over and put out his hand.

"Mighty glad to meet you, Sir. Get much business out here?" The farmer shook his head and grinned.

"Most every wagon stops and I sell plenty." He motioned to the stack of corn.

"Fresh picked this mornin'. Peel one and try it." Charles husked an ear and bit into the juicy kernels.

"Damn good. I'd like a couple bushels."

The other wagons pulled closer and the men came forward. Like Charles, they were sold as soon as they tasted an ear. All together, they bought over a dozen bushels. Charles talked with the old man about his farm. He had come to Nebraska with the rush of farmers that poured into the area to get free land after the Homestead Act of 1862. He and his two sons farmed 160 acres. When the transcontinental railroad began operating he shipped most of his produce to distributors in the east. His fence line ran parallel to the road a few hundred yards toward the river. He loved seeing happy customers and hearing how they liked his corn. The women and children were all chewing on an ear as they pulled away, and they all waved a big goodbye to the old man.

A few days later they passed the point where the river branched to the south. They followed the south fork to a water hole known as Cottonwood Springs where they filled their water barrels. Five more days traveling along the river and they camped at Diamond Springs and stayed over for a day of rest and relaxation. While the children were off playing, Charles sat leaning against the wagon, enjoying a cigar. Looking up at the clouds, he thought about the blue skies of Oregon, the evergreen forests and fertile farmland. Mary was in the wagon mending clothes.

"Be plenty of trees in Oregon," he said. "More trees than you ever saw."

"I know. You always say that. I just want to get there and have a home again."

He drew on his cigar and blew out a big puff of smoke.

"We'll get there alright, and I'll build us a big house like you want. You'll see." She stopped mending and looked out.

"Let's take the girls for a walk," she said. Charles stood up and reached for Alice. Mary climbed down with an arm around Janet. They were as happy as they had been in weeks. In the afternoon, Charles sat on a big rock in front of Mary. She switched the scissors. He looked in her eyes while she clipped his whiskers.

"Be still," she said. "You're as jumpy as a toad."

"Maybe I'll settle down tonight," he said. She leaned back and smiled.

"You will," she said.

In the morning, relaxed and ready, they got back on the road. Twenty miles beyond Diamond Springs, they arrived at the Julesburg Crossing and forded the South Platte River. Their spirits were high as they rolled across the river and onto the trail leading to Courthouse Rock, a famous landmark that helped point the way to Scott's Bluffs. Once used by pony express riders, the road bypassed a rugged stretch of the Oregon Trail that followed the North Platte River.

Oregon Trail River Crossing

There were many rivers to cross on the Oregon Trail, and fording them was difficult and dangerous. Charles usually chose to ford a river rather than pay the fee to cross by a bridge or a ferry.

BEYOND THE BLUFFS

"It's the Courthouse," Charles called out. "Won't be long to the bluffs now." Courthouse Rock rose abruptly above the plain. For two days they traveled toward it, but it never seemed to get closer. On the third day they came to within five miles of it. It stood out on the southern horizon, a huge structure of reddish sandstone that looked like the ruins of an ancient castle; and to its left stood a stone tower called Jailhouse Rock. Like seeing old friends, these guardians of the trail seemed to reach out and touch them.

Charles looked at the sketches in the old journal he carried and compared them with what he saw. Mary looked over his shoulder.

"That man was a pretty good artist," she said.

"Just like he was standing right here where we are," he said. They camped with a view of the two impressive rocks and watched them fade away in the sunset.

The next afternoon they passed Chimney Rock, another unique milestone on the trail. A tapered, chimney-like stone pillar, it rose hundreds of feet from a wide base of rounded rock in the middle of a vast and otherwise empty field, pointing the way to the west. Suddenly they felt surer of themselves. Charles thought of walking out to the chimney, but he was eager to charge ahead.

"If we push hard, we should make the bluffs by tomorrow night," he said.

They were up before dawn and already on their way when sunlight streaked across the plain, stretching long shadows out in front of them. They set a good pace and when they stopped for lunch they could see the bluffs, dimly outlined on the horizon. They hurried on, determined to camp beside Scott's Bluff. It was the tallest and most storied of all the bluffs. It was named after Hiram Scott, a fur trader who died near the bluff in 1828, the year Charles was born. Like approaching a great city, with spires and domes reaching into the clouds, the bluffs rose high above the prairie, dominating the landscape. They looked up at the layers of dusty white, beige and brown rock as they traveled along the south side of the bluffs. When evening shadows darkened the plain and the sun still lit the bluff tops, they pulled up and made camp near the foot of Scott's Bluff.

They stayed by the bluff the following day, resting, hunting and letting the animals graze. The boys ran around catching grasshoppers and chasing lizards. Brother Charles caught a lizard and put it in a jar. Charles went hunting with Bill Jenkins and Tom Brown. They brought back two antelope and dressed them out to roast. Gathered in a circle around the fire, they shared a great feast with the entire party and gave thanks to the Lord. Jack Jarrett got out his banjo and accompanied some Stephen Foster songs. They sang and danced until the moon was high.

On the trail again, they drove through a gap in the bluffs known as Mitchell's Pass and ended the day at Horse Creek, a tributary of the North Platte River. The next day, they entered Wyoming Territory and continued along the North Platte, bound for Fort Laramie. With the harsh Nebraska prairie behind them, and the foothills of the Rocky Mountains ahead of them, a sense of accomplishment mixed with a determination to conquer this new challenge permeated the party. In three days they reached the fort, where they lingered to prepare for the next big test -- reaching and crossing the Continental Divide, defined by the Rocky Mountains. Fort Laramie was a major trading post located at the confluence of the Laramie and North Platte Rivers. It had been a staging point for supplies and troops during the Indian Wars that raged throughout the area in 1876 and part of 1877. Indian leaders Red Cloud and Crazy Horse had surrendered to the army just a few months before their arrival. With the wars over, they proceeded without fear to wash their clothes in the Laramie River, make repairs to the wagons, and let the animals graze in nearby grasslands. It was an uphill grind from Fort Laramie to South Pass, a broad saddle between steep mountain peaks. The oxen needed extra time to rest and build strength for the climb. Although over 7,000 feet high, South Pass was a gentle climb and the only practical way that wagons could cross the divide.

It was the 17th of July when they left Fort Laramie. They were 690 miles from their old Kansas farm -- almost two months on the trail and they were only a third of the way to the Willamette Valley in Oregon. The trail out of Fort Laramie led through rugged hills and broken country to higher ground, where the Sweetwater River joined the North Platte River. Ten days on the trail and they reached Independence Rock in central Wyoming Territory. A long rounded granite outcropping stretching hundreds of yards along the Sweetwater River, it was a favorite camping spot and they were ready for a good riverside rest. Ideally, they would have reached it on July 4th, three weeks earlier. Arriving at that time, a party could be fairly sure of crossing the mountains before it began snowing. Over the years, beginning with the early emigrant trains, hundreds of travelers had stopped to celebrate and carve their names on its sides. In time it became known as the "Register of the Desert." The men climbed around on it and read some of the names.

Leaving Independence Rock, they continued west along the Sweetwater River toward the Rocky Mountains and South Pass. The Sweetwater meandered over a wide range as it flowed from its source in the mountains. To shorten the distance from Fort Laramie to South Pass, the trail crossed the river nine times. The crossings were a nuisance, but the children loved them.

It was early August and they were nearing the summit of South Pass when the season's first snow began to fall. At first it was light and feathery, but a strong wind soon whistled down from the north blowing heavy flakes all across the unprotected sage-tufted pass. In a short time they found themselves in the midst of a blizzard, unable to continue up the slope. They worked the wagons into position to blunt the wind and corralled the animals inside their circle. The temperature dropped well below freezing and they hurried to set up tents and get under cover. It was impossible to build a fire or make supper. Cuddling for warmth, they slept while the wind howled and the snow drifted up against the wagons and around the tents. The morning sun reflected from a vast field of snow with drifts up to two feet deep. Charles looked around the camp.

"We won't be going anywhere today," he said. "Let's hope it warms up and that's the end of it." For the children, it was a perfect time to play. For the adults, it was just another hard time on the road. They cleared a space for a fire and the women put together a big hot breakfast. Spirits were good and the men trudged up the slope to check the condition of the road. They confirmed what Charles believed – best to stay put and wait for the melt. If the melt turned to ice, they would be in serious trouble, but the sun felt warm and it looked like nature was on their side. That night a light snow fell, and they weren't so sure, but the next day was sunny and mild and the snow melted throughout the afternoon. Sage brush appeared where white mounds had been and water trickled down the slope. The following morning they slogged through slush and mud, sometimes getting stuck, but finally able to reach the summit.

It was an occasion to celebrate, but looking west across the uninviting stretch of sand and sagebrush didn't give them much to cheer about. There were buttes, faintly visible in the far distance, but they could see nothing that resembled their vision of the beautiful northwest. Descending the pass they camped at Pacific Springs, the only source of good water they would find for many days, and filled their barrels.

On the flatland below the pass they took a shortcut that led directly to the Green River, a tributary of the Colorado River, in southwest Wyoming Territory. The shortcut saved 50 miles but it was an extremely hard pull across deep sand. It was waterless and forbidding. Earlier travelers had named it the "Little Colorado Desert." When they were within a mile of the Green River, the animals began racing to reach the water. Along with the animals, they splashed in the shallows and rested on the riverbank. The river, too wide and deep to ford, was the most dangerous on the Oregon Trail. They rejoined the main trail and followed it to a ferry landing, where they paid the fee to make a safe crossing.

On the west side of the river, the trail angled northwest into Idaho Territory. It took them a week of hard driving to reach Soda Springs, a welcome place to rest and enjoy drinking the naturally carbonated water that bubbled up from the numerous springs in the area. After a day of rest, they left for the next major stopping point -- Fort Hall, a trading post on the Snake River. Three days later, they made camp at the Fort. They spent two days there to prepare for the long haul to Oregon. Before they left, they had a goodbye party with the Jarretts and their friends. Beyond the Fort, the trail divided into the California

Trail, which turned to the southwest, while the Oregon Trail continued west along the Snake River. At that point the two parties would go their separate ways.

The journey from Fort Hall to the Oregon border tested the endurance of all concerned. Trail-hardened oxen sometimes dropped from exhaustion. It was often difficult to access the river because of the steep walls it had carved into the earth. They ferried across the river at Glenns Ferry and continued northwest to where the Snake River separated Idaho Territory from Oregon State. Here, they ferried the river again and set down at last on Oregon soil. It was September 12, and they had come 1,450 miles.

THE PROMISED LAND

Crossing the Snake River and entering Oregon depressed Mary. They had come so far, suffered so many hardships, and here they were, still facing a desert-like landscape. No great forests, no greenery, just sand and hills dotted with sagebrush spread like a lumpy gray carpet before them. She complained.

"*This* is your promised land?"

'It gets better, lots better," Charles told her. "A few weeks more and you'll see the beauty of it."

They traveled about 15 miles across a dry and treeless stretch. The trail took them to Keeney Pass, the divide between the Snake and Malheur Rivers. Dark mountains were visible far to the north. In a broad swale between hills covered with brown grass and skimpy clumps of brush, they made camp. Another dry and dusty 10 miles and they reached the Malheur River. They camped in a pleasant patch of willow trees near the river. The men built a fine fire with wood from the willows. The next day, Mary, Janie and Rosemary went to the river and washed clothes. In good spirits, they came up from the river with baskets of clean laundry. Dried in the sun and freshened by the wind off the river, their clothes smelled good for the first time in weeks.

Driving from near dawn to dusk the next day, they made camp at Birch Creek, about 20 miles to the north. The next day they camped at Farewell Bend, where the trail approached the west side of the Snake River, and then continued northwest into the Burnt River Canyon. The clear water of the Burnt River rolled through the canyon between bald and blackened hills, their dark color the result of frequent grass fires. They could smell ashes from a recent fire that had burned across the road and down to the river. It was slow going where the trail skirted steep hillsides with little room to spare. On September 19th, they emerged from the canyon and made camp on a brushy plain called Pleasant Valley. Far to the northwest, beyond the nearby hills, they could see the Blue Mountains, and many mountain peaks stood out on the western horizon.

For three days they traveled north through the Powder River Valley. Near Ladd Creek they camped by a large pond of steaming saltwater that was hot enough to use for cooking. The next day they drove into the Grande Ronde River valley and camped by the river. There was good grass and they rested a day while the animals grazed. After crossing the river they started an extremely hard pull through the Blue Mountains. The oxen struggled to keep their footing on the steep, rocky trail. Mary got down and walked beside the wagon, carrying baby Janet in one arm and leading Alice with the other. Charles strapped as much as he could on the horses to lighten the load, and the older children carried buckets of smaller things, but halfway up one slope the wagon stopped. His team could go no further. He pulled on the brake and walked back to see Jenkins. His team had also bogged down.

"We'll have to double up," Charles said. "With two teams on a wagon, I think we can make it."

"Okay, Charlie, let's give it a try." They walked the Jenkins team to the front and hitched it up. With a crack of the whip and powerful commands, the wagon began to move. When Charles' wagon was on relatively level ground, they unhitched the eight oxen and walked them back to the Jenkins wagon. Jenkins made it to the top and then they took his team back to add to Tom's wagon. It took a good three hours before all three wagons got to higher ground. The next challenge was a steep drop down into a valley, and then another climb as bad as the first. Late in the day they made camp in a pine forest where the trail flattened out. Mary loved the clean fragrance of pine and gathered a bucket of needles to carry in the wagon.

The following day they reached the small mountain community of Meacham, Oregon, where they learned that homesteads were being taken up around the town of Weston, about 20 miles northeast of Pendleton. Jenkins thought it might be a good place to settle and asked about the land. A rolling sandy area, it was excellent for growing wheat, peaches and apricots. As they continued through the mountains he talked it over with Tom and Charles. They were set on continuing on to the Willamette Valley and encouraged Jenkins to come along, but after another day on the trail he had made up his mind – he would go to Weston.

Beyond Meacham, they crossed Deadman Pass and coming down the west side of the Blue Mountains they could see Mt. Hood, snow-white and majestic in the Cascade Mountain Range. At Pendleton, on the Umatilla River, the three families camped together for the last time. Tom was related to John Downing, who lived near Sublimity, a town in the Willamette Valley about 16 miles southeast of Salem. They had come 1,645 miles and it would be another 300 miles before they reached Sublimity. It was excellent farming country, known for the big red apples and juicy berries that grew there, and that was where he and Charles intended to settle. He gave Jenkins the address.

"Let's keep in touch and see how things work out."

"Good idea, Tom."

Mary and Janie hated to see Rosemary go.

"I hope we'll see each other again," Mary said. "When we get settled in the valley, you could come for a visit and we could go see the ocean together."

"I would love that," Rosemary said. The three women had become extremely close, and they cried their goodbyes.

A final farewell and Jenkins started up the road along the Wildhorse River, on his way to Weston. The others watched and waved until the wagon disappeared beyond a rise in the road. A little later, Charles and Tom pulled out and continued traveling west across open prairie land. They stopped for lunch by a spring. It was a clear day, and far across the prairie they could see the peaks of mountains in the Cascade Range.

"The other side of those mountains and we'll be there," Charles said. "Thirty years ago they called it the 'Promised Land' and it still is."

"But how did they ever make it back then? We can barely make it now." Mary said.

"It's like we read about........what you worried about. Hundreds of folks did die trying, but times are better for us. There's still some hard road ahead, but we're through most of the worst."

"Thank God. I've already seen enough for a lifetime."

That night they camped near a Umatilla River crossing, a good spot to rest, let the animals graze and wash clothes. Charles and Tom went hunting and came back with a pair of geese. Roast goose had everyone licking their fingers at supper. With the children in bed, Charles took Mary for a walk in the moonlight. It was cool and the air was clear. They spread a blanket near the river and sat looking up at the stars.

"Beautiful night," he said. And just then a silver streak cut across the sky. It seemed to hit the moon and come out the other side.

"Never saw that before!" They studied the sky and before long they saw two more meteors. Mary sometimes complained about the trials of the trail, but there under the starry sky she admitted that there were things she really liked about the west. Charles tried to encourage her.

"It's hard out here alright, harder than I thought, but we're making it. You know we're making it, and we'll be better than ever," he said. Their faces seemed to glow in the soft light of the moon and Charles saw stars in her eyes. He leaned back and gently pulled her to his chest. She sighed and snuggled against him. He rocked her in his arms and rolled her onto the ground. Somewhere across the river a coyote howled, but they didn't hear it.

They camped another day while the women did some mending, the children played and the men did maintenance on the wagons. Fresh and ready for the road, they broke camp early in the morning, drove 12 miles, forded Butter Creek, and made camp. It was the last stop for good water until they reached Willow Creek, two days later. Another two days and they camped beside the John Day River. They were drawing ever closer to the mighty Columbia River. Beyond the John Day they came to the Deschutes River, another big tributary of the Columbia. They crossed the river and traveled on to The Dalles, a town on the Columbia River where river boats ran west to Oregon City. To continue overland travel they began a long and difficult drive south on Barlow Road. The road led across a valley and up through rugged hills around the southern flanks of Mt. Hood.

Three days down the road, they camped in a meadow and let the animals build strength for the climb to Barlow Pass. They had a magnificent view of the symmetrical glacier-covered mountain rising high above the Cascade foothills. Many deer visited the edges of the meadow. Charles and Tom went hunting, and for several days they had venison steaks for supper.

On October 15th they reached Barlow Pass. At over 4,000 feet in altitude, the road crossed a divide in the Cascade Mountain

Range. Icy winds swept down from Mt. Hood and there were freezing nights. Fortunately, they got through the pass and down the west side of the mountains before it began snowing. Continuing around the base of Mt. Hood they followed the Sandy River to the northwest, spending one day fishing and washing clothes. They crossed the Sandy River three times. The road turned to the southwest at the third crossing and led to the Clackamas River. After crossing the Clackamas, they finally reached the end of the Oregon Trail -- Oregon City.

Magnificent Mount Hood

*Mount Hood is one of the highest peaks in the Cascade
Mountain Range. Its rugged features dominate
much of Oregon's central skyline.
Reaching the end of the Oregon Trail included the challenge
of skirting the base of the mountain.
A dormant volcano, its last eruption occurred just a few
years after Charles led his wagon around it.*

At Home in Oregon

Reaching Oregon City took an effort greater than anything the two families had ever experienced. And now, with the daunting mountains, rivers and prairies behind them, they celebrated for two days. They had survived every hard day on the trail without injury and only minor sickness among them. Charles and Tom visited the General Land Office to get current information about homesteading in the Willamette Valley. What they learned was discouraging. They came away with homestead application forms and directions to the few places where farmland was still available. Concerned, but determined to succeed in their quest to find good land and make a new beginning, they started south on the road to Sublimity.

The first day out, they crossed the Molalla River and continued southwest to the Pudding River. They passed many farms with groves of hazelnuts and wide fields of green grass. They followed the Pudding River to the south, stopping several times to visit with farmers, learn about crops and ask directions to unclaimed land. As they had been told at the Land Office, there was little land available along the river. They did find one piece on the side of a hill that sloped sharply to the river. They camped there for a day and did some fishing. The land offered a good view of the river and plenty of trees, but it was not fit for farming. The Oregon countryside was beautiful, but Charles began wondering if he was too late to find a good claim.

"Surely there's something for us," he told Mary. "Surely there is." She read the disappointment in his voice and the furrows in his face and tried to encourage him.

"We'll be alright. We'll find a place and we'll be fine."

"Further south, maybe," he said.

In early November, they arrived at the Downing farm. None of the available land they had seen on the way showed the kind of promise that Charles had dreamed about. The Downings welcomed the two families and offered them space in their barn. This would have to do until they found places to settle. After nearly six months of life on the trail, staying in a barn was almost a luxury. The Downing family helped them get settled and ready for the winter. Mrs. Downing arranged a spare room in the house where the little ones could stay at night. She was glad to have company. The wives spent hours together, sharing chores and looking after the children. As soon as he could, Charles started looking for work and found a part-time job with a local cabinet maker. In his free time he scouted the area looking for a place to homestead. Everywhere he looked the good land had already been claimed. Then a letter addressed to Tom, care of Mr. Downing, arrived. It was from Jenkins who reported that he had acquired a good homestead and was beginning to establish himself. With little demand for carpenters in the Willamette Valley, Charles considered going to Weston and applying for a homestead. That night he wrote to Jenkins and explained his situation. In a dark mood, he confessed his frustration to Mary.

"It's not like I thought," he said. "Everything's gone! We can't make it here. I'm thinking I'll ride to Weston and find Jenkins."

Feeling his hurt, she listened patiently.

"We'll make it," she whispered. "We've come all this way. I know we will." With their arms around each other, they stood in silence.

And so, Charles left his family and traveled by horseback to Weston, a pioneer village tucked between rolling hills where grasslands waved in the wind. He filed for a homestead near the Jenkins property and went to work at carpentry. There was an epidemic of smallpox and scores of people were dying. Dozens of coffins were needed and he helped build them. His homestead was granted, but, after digging three dry wells, he relinquished his right to the land and got a claim to harvest timber in the Blue Mountains. This proved to be worthwhile. He built a small cabin where he could live while he worked the timber. He continued to search for a place to settle and build a home for the family. In luck, he acquired an abandoned homestead with a good spring and began building a house with lumber from his mountain property.

When the smallpox epidemic had passed and he had a good start on the house, he wrote to Mary Jane and told her he would come and get the family.

"It's good here," he wrote. "I'm building a house for us and I'll come for you soon."

On a sunny September afternoon, Charles pointed ahead to the road leading into Weston. Golden leaves fluttered on the poplar trees that lined the road.

"That's our town," he said to Mary. "And wait till you see our land!" He turned the wagon onto a lane that curved up a gentle grade.

"There she is!" he said. Mary looked at the unfinished house and tears filled her eyes.

"Oh, Charlie!" she said. "It's beautiful!"

"And plenty big," he said. "Two fireplaces and rooms upstairs for the kids."

They pulled up to the house, and little Janet ran to the porch with her brothers and sisters. Waving their arms in the air, they jumped up and down on the rough wooden planks and screamed.

"We're Home!"

Manufactured by Amazon.ca
Acheson, AB